Introduction:

I have suffered for a long time now with severe depression, especially after my medical separation from my life in the United States military. On the outside I am physically fit despite some extra hardware and I am hygienic, I get along with others, I am relatively successful. I am also the one my friends go to when they are having issues in their lives.

On the inside though...

I am at war.

I teeter on the precipice of the point of no return. My thoughts are overwhelmingly negative, nd I am burning out. With these ensuing pages, I intend to leave the shadows and, reluctantly, share a side of me that only the closest in my life even have an inkling of knowledge about. I get through the darkest days by writing.

Soliloquy of a Savage: Slaying Demons with Words is part one in a series of silent emotional utbursts, rants and mental blood lettings. An attempt at a literary exorcism. I release the pressure I am feeling on to the page and leave it there. This is my way of letting some of the demons that claw and writhe within me out, and into the world. I am TRULY terrified to share these words, as they will permanently change the views that my loved ones and peers have of me. These words can potentially uin future opportunities for me within my professional field. I feel, however, that by not releasing this detritus I am living a lie and wasting my own words.

Hopefully I can help or inspire another lost soul, damaged being, and hopelessly disconnected human, or desperate fighter battling with their own demons. To become better, stronger and more courageous.

Thank you so much for sharing your time with me.

-Adam

To Be Honest...

I am a father to 2 amazing boys, a husband to a beautiful, strong woman, a brother, a son, an uncle and a loyal friend. I am a veteran; a proud warrior and fighter. I am strong, fit, and capable despite sustained injuries. My life is amazing. I'm young, and more successful in so many ways and infinitely more so than I deserve.

I am also deeply flawed. I am consumed by a ravenous, insatiable maelstrom that keeps me, perpetually, treading water. I seek peace through exercise, hard work and suffering; strength through wounding. In private, I stumble under the weight of the universe. My range of emotions, like the tides, ebb and flow from elation to rage to sadness and finally numbness before the loneliness and exhaustion overtake me like a pack of starved wolves and I finally shut down. I am terrified that people will see the fear, instability and the feral, rabid confusion in my eyes. I hide behind muscles, false smiles and direct, with purpose, movement. I wear confidence like a suit of armor. I always feel on edge; like I'm about to explode and all this hate, anxiety, fear, anger, passion and love that the maelstrom devours will regurgitate, flood and drown all that I cherish.

In all of this internal turmoil and darkness, I am forced to find my strength. I am forced to focus on the task at hand. You see, when you are forced to keep going, to keep ahead of the impending doom; you can really master your craft. You are forced to focus on that flickering light in the dark that represents the things in your life that make you *want* to keep going. I started this book with the best in my life, because in order to combat the depression and the anxiety, I have to constantly remind myself of why I want to keep going. Why I work so hard in every aspect of my life. Why I must set an example for my sons, and have the strength to be the man and husband that my wife wants and occasionally needs. To remember that I am a warrior and a fighter, that I have an obligation to all, and to whom I care about.
This is me. Scars, and all.

When the wolves close in; turn the suffering into strength, take a step back and kick them, one by one, in the fucking teeth until they retreat.

Drifting.

The older that I get, the emptier that I feel. The less, satisfied. The less fulfilled... intellectually, physically and spiritually. I feel numb most of the time. I feel like I am trapped in an outer-body experience. I can almost see myself from afar as I move through the motions of this modern existence. Pretending to be human. Glassy eyes, and thoughtlessly placed limbs... grabbing my steering wheel for my commute, pushing the cart for my pre-packaged sustenance. Wasting it. Fainting half-smiles at other half-lives. If this is existing; I don't want to exist. It could all burn down and it would not mean a thing to me. I don't feel hate, or contempt anymore. Nor' do I feel love, lust or happiness. I am the Anti-Man. I am what I feel. Nothing. I am stuck on re-run. I *do* feel homesick for a place that I'm not sure exists. Where I am now doesn't feel right, nor' does the place I came from. I wish for a coma, so that I could live within my own mind.

I catch myself all of the time. Going dead when around friends and family. I hide behind perpetual exhaustion. The symptoms are the same. As long as I continue to grind myself to the bone, I can hide.

As dramatic as it sounds, I can't remember the last time I've been myself. I don't ever show the real me. I show the drunk me, the actor, the mime, the great pretender.

The only time I let anything out is in my writings. These words of mine are the escape points for the pressure that builds within a reactor.

Every day is ground zero.

No Man's Land

I got stuck inside my head tonight; again. I had to stay in there and fight; again. I wanted to call you to help me get out, but you always get annoyed. The emptiness. The void. The hollow skin suit that I wear becomes ridiculously over-sized. I want to wander off and never return. Swim towards the horizon. Shed my man suit to the flesh, muscles and tendons. The humanity. If I can keep digging this hole, maybe it will finally get too deep for me to climb out, and the dirt too high for anyone to get in it with me. I just hope that the persona I leave behind is the right one.

Bring on the numbness. No fear. No worries. No anxiety. No expectations. No goals. No crowds, or social obligations. No more anything. I'm going back into my head, and going to war.

Back to No Man's Land.

Blood & Vinegar.

The sleepless nights. The anger. The sadness. The bad, consuming thoughts. The daily spells of dizziness.

Happiness evades me. Contentment is unattainable to me.

Money, friends, family... it is not enough. I am a miserable, angry, insatiable piece of damaged flesh. I pay the man daily with my failures and weaknesses, my blood and sweat, and the man is just as insatiable as me.

I no longer care about my long-term health, or future.

I cannot wait to escape this planet.

The longer that I am here; the more feral that I am becoming. The less human connection, empathy... simple fucks to give. I am almost a rabid liability to myself and those around me. I can hardly contain the monster within. My chest hurts, my head spins, and my body catches fire. I get physically ill.

I have been focusing on my raw power. My pain tolerance. Callus upon callus, self-induced bloodletting, runic scars. I am readying myself to be a worthy sacrifice.

I will go where the lost minds go.

Focus. Divert.

I am so tired of my body failing me.

I wish that I could just cut off the useless limbs.

When parts of my body hurt too much to use; to lift even light weight.

I buckle over, it feels like I am being hit with a bolt of lightning.

The impotence of my limbs negate all good from earlier in the day.

I do not have a stop button, so I go, go, go in all of my destructive glory.

As it stands, I do not intend to grow old.

The body can only take so much before it completely fails, and living does not become worth it.

I love and accept the pain because I have to.

It is all I know anymore.

I will continue to embrace the pain until the pain finally wins.

I can barely use my left arm and hand as I type this.

I am in survival mode.

No literary embellishments.

No creativity.

No fancy words or phrases.

Just black and white.

Straight words.

Writing to focus the brain on something else.

Focus and Divert.

Random Mental Detritus

This life. The mortgage, the cars, the false worth of college degrees and the debt that goes with them, the uniforms; suits and ties, handshakes and fake smiles, the 9 to 5… it's a fucking death sentence. Comfort and convenience; ball and chain.

The loneliness attacks me randomly. It rips at my flesh, and leaves me to bleed out.

Exhaustion. The sky is a crashing type of anxiety. My hands shake and tremble uncontrollably. My mind checks out. Lost. This kind of life is all consuming. I work in the fire. I can feel the heat, but it does not turn me to ash. To survive this, you must be hard; inside and out. There is nothing but honesty here. You either make the cut, or you ARE cut. I've worked so hard to get here.

I am teetering on the precipice of a downward spiral like none I could ever have imagined. I've never been this terrified, or this helpless. My scalpel is on its way. I'll bleed out before I ever hit the ground.

This weight on my chest… it's too much. I'm fighting this desire to destroy myself. To just get it over with through self-ruination.

The anxiety comes in waves. It hits hard, and takes chunks out of me. It's like getting repeatedly attacked by a bear. I'm so afraid of losing my heart, and mind. I don't want to become cold, and hard. Death is slowly becoming an option. I can't live like this. I will not live as a failure. A failure as a Husband, Father, and Man. The three things I want so badly to be great at. I'd rather perish with honor; I will leave this world alive.

The clawing, gnashing, mashing of my insides is becoming too hard to handle. My head is breaking, even worse my heart. My heart… I'm not sure how much longer I can last; feeling desperate.

The depression rips my insides apart. Sometimes the weight is unbearable. I wish to die in my sleep. I try to talk about it, but I'm not listened to. I can taste the charring of what's left; rage replaces love. Regret, and longing replace what's in front of me. The monsters have been clawing for so long, I have become one.

I can feel the walls closing in on me. My body is overwhelmed with anxious heat. I reach out needing help, and I am shut down.

I am not sure how much longer I can pretend to not be dead inside. This lack of human touch is pushing me deeper into a darkness that I have been running from for too long.

I want to burn the planet. Watch its garbage inhabitants turn to ash before my eyes. I want to turn it all to black.

I am sick of feeling like a fucking joke. My disconnection endures. This life continues to be unbearable. I feel like a stranger in my own home.

The fire, hate, and fury festers deep within me. I can feel it charring my insides. My body perspires as I hold back the magma. Tunnel vision takes over, and my teeth grind. I want to burn all of humanity alive. No quarter given to anyone.

You know what rips, and tears at my insides and makes me physically ill? Keeping up with the quo. Violence? No problem. Natural disaster? No problem. Putting up with the bumbling, self-righteous, androgynous masses of this land? Now, that is a test. A mass group of humans with no identities. White noise, and static in physical form. Whiners, and hypocrites. High I.Q.'s, and no values. You can dish it out 24/7, but crumble into trembling idiots once confronted. It's shameful. It's an affront to your much more capable primate cousins. It's the same in every direction. I can't wait for the implosion, so that my kind can run through you; smashing your participation trophies along the way.

Even at my best. Even when everything could not be better. The demons, these ghosts, they pound and claw at my insides. My years of bitter resolve, and layers of scar tissue hold back their relentless pursuit of my consumption. My very existence travels with entropy along the event horizon of the black hole that I was born with.

My mind has been trying real hard to check out. The only way I know how to keep it check is to bombard it with information.

I continue to push knowing that I will never, no matter how bad I want to, live a normal existence. I will never feel fully human, or completely comfortable among others. I will look at my wife, and children, and I will long to be what I am supposed to be; what they deserve. I have never felt human. I will always have a disconnection with others.

The loneliness attacks me randomly. It rips at my flesh, and leaves me to bleed out.

The separation continues, perpetuating the ever present loneliness. I try so hard to feel like one of them…one of you, but at every junctur

I realize how different I am, and the pull of my ancestors continues to tighten. Every day I feel more, and more out of place among the modern human.

The older I grow, the more out of place I feel. I find very little in common with the majority of these humans. They are sloppy, loud, weak and clumsy.

The further I can get from these humans, the better.

I feel like a caged Animal. I look at mindless humans, and feel fucking stupid that I was somehow tricked into their zoo.

Inside of me there is a perpetual storm. It is heaving with violence, discontent, and tattered dreams. I avoid making eye contact for too long, as to hide the storm from others. If one were to see the monster inside of me pounding furiously to escape from behind my eyes, I would be exiled out of fear, and ignorance. The war rages on, and I am forced to watch from this side of the line, until the battles start to bleed over. Then I'll let the monster out, and be who I was born, and trained to be.

It feels like my body is rejecting my soul. So much discomfort.

The exhaustion, and loneliness exact their heavy weight. All I know to do is grind, and grind. At one point I'll be just dust, and the universe can have me back.

My sanity and my insanity are interlocked in a waltz to the grinding muse of decay.

The more I hear humans the less human I feel. I want to be bigger, stronger, smarter, and more brutal than the average human. I have the injuries of a Warrior, and that spirit never dies. I cannot stomach the perpetual waste of movement, breath, and space human's exhibit. All their superfluous noise, and actions. I wish I lived in a time where I could run through them, alas! They are so weak that they must be protected at all times by their laws. I am a beast among citizens. Someday this world will shift, and my kind will creep out of the shadows, and survive on our savagery.

My brain never turns off. My eyes ache with perpetual exhaustion, my body wears the weight of sleepless nights, and the impending doom breathes its righteous breath down my throat.

Mankind… you have been on the brink of war since your inception. Disaster looms on a planetary scale; just a slight nudge, and we're all in the shit. The omens are all around us. In between the lines, in the shadows, and boiling over on the back burners. The thing about war is that it never stays silent or hidden. War will come quickly, and decisively like blood from a nicked artery, and it will encompass all of mankind. Ignorance is bliss, until the truth kicks in your door, and drags you into the street half dressed, cold and scared.

My quest for knowledge consumes me. Maybe it is my way of filling the human abyss, or keeping my mind off my mind. The math never ceases. The words are a perpetual onslaught of accumulated Latin, and Germanic translations, evolution, and articulations. My brain devours my heart, and takes over the star dust. Sleep is nothing but an undulation in the process. I am evolving. I look up into the eyes of the galaxy, and know this earthly Purgatory is not my home.

I have lost my passion. It's been fading like the final light rays from a long dead star. I look at the things that once drove me from the shell that I reside in, and I feel nothing for them. My desires are faint, and brutishly realistic. My chest burns with contempt.

Sleep is a skilled strategist. It out maneuvers, out flanks, and stays ahead of every countermeasure that I can think of. **The Art of Snore.**

Loneliness.

It is dark, and constant free falling.

It is the sound of familiar, yet foreign, voices, and the echo of your own footsteps as you chase yourself.

It is making eye contact with yourself in the mirror, and seeing a stranger.

It is knowing you're loved, yet not getting to feel it.

It is wanting to feel. To feel anything constantly. To welcome excessive pain, anger, happiness, excitement, fear and sadness; knowing the feeling will last just long enough to leave you craving more.

It is living in your own shadow.

It is Purgatory, before Hell.

It is never enough, yet too much to carry.

It is wishing death, accepting death, and hoping for more life.

The exhaustion. The fear. The emptiness. The slithering insides, and the demon's unrelenting claws.

It is a waiting game.

Depression.

The Mirror.

Waking up and seeing that stranger in the mirror. The blue eyes, stained with red, and yellow. The colors of personal abuse and neglect. Far too young for crow's feet. Far too young for this amount of scars. This amount of fears. Far too young to want to escape this life. Far too old, though, to not know. To know better. To care so much about the wrong things. Too old to knowingly feed the wolves. To sacrifice ones flesh to the hunger and the habits. To wish for an end to it all. To wish for the great implosion. Ground Zero.

It would be better this way.

Everything is always just out of reach. Even sound seems to be a beat too far ahead to register. Marching on to four/four time and stumbling two-by-two, face down in the dust, scabs tearing, blood dripping and collecting at the feet.

It's called breaking even.

Treading water may not be drowning, but it's definitely not swimming. The feet are desperately kicking, the muscles burn and cramp. My arms feel like lead, and the thought of letting that weight just take the body to the bottom starts to overtake the survival response. Exhaustion whispers in the ears, and tells you to let go… you close your eyes and drift… **WAKE UP!**

Sweat. Bleed. Suffer.

Listen to others. Feed the wolves in secrecy. Smile at everyone you meet. Support those who need you. Cry alone and in privacy. Keep the surges of raw emotion to the paper.

Suppress. Accommodate. Annihilate.

It all gets kept inside of me. 99% of the demons, ghosts, the wounds, stress, phobias. The perpetual internal bleeding seen, by only me, in the sink and the toilet, the shower floor… and the mirror.

Deliberate Breathing.

Happiness absolutely eludes my grasp. I reach for it, and it falls through my fingers like the fine sands of the Middle East; leaving just enough dust in the cracks of my hands to remind me that it actually exists.

The consuming weight of just existing pushes down on every cell in my body. I can physically feel it. I feel it everywhere. My arms, my legs, shoulders, back and organs. I am never comfortable. My joints ache, and I am permeated with exhaustion. It feels like I am always wading into the current through a shallow river.

I find solace knowing that I will get to die someday. Death sounds peaceful; nice. When I lay down to try and sleep, I pretend that I am bleeding out. My whole body grows colder as the blood leaves my body, all the weight slides off of me, and I breathe slow and long; deliberate. I close my eyes, and take one last long, hot breath out of my nose. My pursed lips separate with a subtle, damp pop, and my jaw *finally* relaxes, then I pass on. I sleep.
In silence, and away from others.

However, I always wake up, usually only a couple of hours later, and it is back to the weight, the sadness, and exhaustion. The deadlines, traffic, humans and garbage. It is back to despondently grasping into the sandy wind, and a life made up of affectation; disguised smiles, forced conversations, customary interactions, and fake excitement.

Back to the living.

Backburner Thoughts

There is a precipice that I precariously teeter upon between anguish and triumphant elation. A grey hairline fracture from falling in either direction.

The past keeps its teeth firmly planted in my flesh.

The past. All of the lone, long, late night, and directionless walks... all of the familiar landmarks stand as testaments of what could have... should have been. The sound of my footsteps echo off of the fences that I pass. I get caught up in the cobwebs of my thoughts; cobwebs that should have been swept from the corners of my mind long ago. I feel like I am lost and adrift in space. Doomed and alone with the jagged detritus of my thoughts.
Time does not heal. It reminds. It nags. It perpetually rings in my ears like tinnitus. It slowly consumes. It alienates.

I want to feel close. I want to be worthy. I want to feel human. I want the sadness to surrender. I want to be excited for the morning... I want to be able to sleep. I want to be more than a caricature, more than a persona. I wish I could leave my masks in the closet and just be what I am. To replace the rotting fruit that makes up my insides... with anything else.

I do not feel casual emotions. I hate, murderously. I fall in love; tragic Shakespearean, hard to breathe love. I get happy... too fucking happy. I get sad... too fucking sad. None of these emotions.. these feelings last long. They get swallowed, almost as fast as they appeared, in a numb, cold fog. Leaving me standing there, in the middle, empty and maniacally clawing to get them back.

I know that I am just weak. Too weak to defeat the avalanches of anxiety. Too weak to embrace what I have as success. Too weak to fill the void. Too weak to lift the weight of this depression. Too weak to truly change. Too weak to sweep the cobwebs and remove the teeth from my flesh.

At one point I will have to look over the precipice and take the leap.

The Beauty of Isolation

True strength is found in isolation.

In loneliness. In the sound of your own mind.

In isolation what you do, what you accomplish is pure and true. To sweat and bleed in solitude is as close to the gods as one can get. To exist, alone, in a feral state behind the lines that separate man from animal; cold, wet hyper-alert and content.

It is pure honesty. Alone; there are no lies, no exaggerations and no illusions. **You are what and who you are.** To thrive in isolation takes a deep, and ancient understanding of your soul. To know yourself beyond the clothes you wear, the company that you keep, the job title that you, so precariously hold, or the available funds in your bank account.

Isolation and discipline are brother and sister.

It takes discipline to exist in isolation. To push yourself under your own will. No spectators, no one to admire your efforts, or accomplishments, no one to tell your stories, or praise your deeds.

When alone, you are the Alpha and the Omega. You are all that exists. Your gods are all that exist. Your demons, your devils… your fears and delights. They are yours, and yours alone.

If you are weak in isolation then you are truly weak. If you can't control your urges, your hunger, or your laziness… then **you are what you are.**

Nothing else matters. What your loved ones think of you, what your peers think of you are smoke and mirrors. Isolation is the great truth, Discipline is the great equalizer. Brother and sister know.

You know.

One and Two and Three.

Repeat.

It is a long, exhausting and bloody journey. The light at the end of the tunnel is faint and fleeting; the way coagulated vitreous dances its shadow across your retina. Was it even ever there at all? Footsteps march to the cadence of your heart beat. Just one more step. Just one more step. Keep breathing. In. Out. In. Out.

Bad thoughts. Heavy dreams.

The earthy, metallic taste of lead, dust and blood fills your mouth, throat and lungs. The sun is relentless and heavy. Nightfall can't come soon enough. You are safest under the stars. A shivering lump in the darkness. Your teeth chattering and your ears buzzing. Swollen joints. Cracked lips. Black fingernails. The weight of the universe resting on your shoulders. Some experiences stick with you. Some ravenously rip parts of you away, and some possess you. Turns you into a monster. Turns you against yourself. Makes you wonder what happened to you. Turns you into a stranger. Makes you hate yourself. Keeps you at war. Keeps you wanting war: It kills you.

Silence.

The speedometer reads 80. I look to my left... 85... to my right... I am so fucking tired 95. I look straight ahead... 100... the world in front of me fades to black as my eyes close. I let go of the wheel, my shoulders relax and my hands slump and lay idly to my sides. My long endured joint pain is forgotten. My jaw loses its long held clinch and my teeth finally separate, I can feel my breath, calm and smooth exiting through my mouth. I know there is nothing left to do. I can feel the lines on the road vibrate my car, then the rhythm of the dirt I stay fully relaxed. Not a thought on my mind. My eyes remain gently closed. The sound of twisting metal. Glass shattering. The exorcism is violent and quick. I feel nothing. I am free.

March

I don't want to own anything anymore.

Not anymore.

I want to punish the sky. I want to punish the water and send my fists through the Earth.

To exist in the void.

I am the universe. The singular moment of me. All that exists.

Blood, tissue, tendons and bone, and muscle. The churning inferno that makes up my brain.

Control is an illusion.

Happiness, contentment, sorrow; all of it. Dust and ash. A brief exhalation. Nothingness.

All that truly exists.

The only thing that is real is the Beast.

The blood lust. The cold. The fire. The grinding and gnashing of filed teeth.

Blood. Sweat. The wide alert eyes and the shallow, rapid, focused breaths of both predator and prey.

There is no freedom in humanity.

Shed your skin and abandon it along with your dirty clothes.

Strength comes through wounding.

Freedom spawns from defeat.

From the precipice. From the void.

EXORCISMS

HE.

He could feel the crescendo of the heat from the blood as it snaked its way down his arms, and saturated the cuffs of his dress shirt. His teeth ground flat from years of grinding them. His nails chewed to the cuticle. His fists are hard though. His arms muscular, his body scarred and his empathy wasted. He does not hate; he is passed hate. He is utilitarian; granite. Like the stones that litter his home town. The fat fuck sat next to him at the bar, profusely sweating while ineffectually hitting on the waitress; he reeked of fried food, failure and impotence.

He is tired of the lazy, and the in the way. The obese and pointless. He prays to the gods for an equalizer. An E.M.P. … anything. He is so tired of having to bite his tongue, and hold back his instincts. He is tired of watching the weak, and destructive shit on this planet. The bible-pushers and the salesmen. The liberals and the right-wing. There is no left and here is no right to him. He curses the cures of modern man. Let the weak, sick and incapable die off! Let them eat and drink themselves to death. Let them kill each other off. Let them eat each other. HE continues to harden himself in solitude.

With every news story, every red light, every human that gets in his way; he loses even more of himself. He truly hates the human race. Every interaction is excruciating. The more they speak, move, and idle about, he loses more and more. He further recedes and the less he wants to keep existing here.

To him; this is a survival situation: The 9 to 5. The commute. The grocery stores, strip malls, and public eateries. Every day he is forced to dig deeper and deeper. It's to the point of self-consumption.

He sees the manipulative paint schemes, hears the white-noise that drifts through public spaces… all the pacifiers of the rabid human species.

He trains and waits.

Record Keeping.

0230: Chest pain. The welling up of tears. Feelings of loss and longing for non-existent moments.

0233: Boisterous laughter. Chest pain.

0301: Sadness. Deep and Legit.

0357: Fury and Exercise… Immense Pain.

0400: Hundreds of pushups. Hundreds of squats. Need heavier weights.

0540: Sweat and Exhaustion. Peace.

17 Aug 19 (part 2)

2300: Severe depression. Called my wife and woke her up. She was too tired to talk. I apologized and let her go.

2312: Sadness. A flash of rage. Sadness.

2349: Wishing that I was better at everything. Falling in slow motion.

18 Aug 2019

0011: Feeling violent. Miss the sweat and blood… and chaos of hand to hand. Need someone who can push me. Who is a legitimate threat. Fists and handshakes.

0110: Training. Always training. 7 Days a Week. I will never be satisfied. I will never be strong enough. Deadly enough. Skilled and fit enough. Capable enough. I do not care about possessions. I do not care about money, or titles. The only thing that matters is what is accomplished, alone, in the shadows. Sweat equity. Blood equity. I ma not always be the most "successful" in the room, but I will ALWAYS be the most dangerous.

This is what keeps me disciplined. Keeps me clean and calloused.

0250: Hundreds of reps. Liters of sweat. A little bit of B Neg. Zero emotions. CLEAN.

0328: Turned up the fan to suppress the buzzing in my ears; really need to stop biting my nails.

0528: Ready to attempt sleep, and give my body a chance to recover from the abuse. Every sleep cycle I wake up less human, and that's the way I like it. I harbor no jealousy, no guilt, and no falsities. I compare myself to no one, but the creature in the mirror. There is no waste here.

Sleep well demons.

Forged.

Exhaustion is real. It is deep, and all consuming. It compounds the weight of the world and, like a hammer on an anvil, crushes and crushes and crushes.

The fire inside stokes the coals of the forge and in the process turns his insides to ash. It is all held in with the stacked on scar tissue and strained, torn muscles of a warrior fighting the ghosts of a long over war.

He was taken out of the fight, but refuses to lay down his arms, to let his eyes and sore body rest, to unclench his calloused fists, or stop grinding his teeth in anticipation of the next attack.

His enemy has no face. No battle strategy. No end game. He knows that he cannot win, but he treads water anyways. He superfluously swings into the wind, and pushes with all his might against the sky and the Earth. He embraces the pain. The discomfort. The frustration and the numbness.

He finds his peace in the knowledge that he is in this for himself, also that he will not win. He leaves his fingernails in the dirt. His blood, sweat and tears in the flood waters. His hopes are long gone. His life is measured in breaths and footsteps.

With his mere existence.

His main battle strategy is defiance. Resilience. The disconnection of being something other than human. Being born from the fire and ash. He knows of his impending doom. He embraces it.

He looks forward to returning to the eternal forge.

A Short Truth.

I believe in honesty. True honesty. Self-honesty.

No exaggerations. No excessive talk. No comparisons. No illusions.

I believe in sweat and blood.

A true knowledge of oneself.

I believe in callouses and scars.

RESULTS.

If it comes from the mouth it does not count. Words are worthless. Stories are just stories. No one cares. The more you talk the less you say.

There are no exceptions in my world.

You do the work. It shows.

Be More Than Human

Why be a pack animal? Easily herded, corralled and eaten? Why be content in your own body? Why not strive for something stronger, bigger and harder to kill?

Why be human?

True freedom comes when fear is gone. When you can walk tall and mighty, supported by strong capable legs, and a formidable upper body; like an oak among dogwoods.

A bear among coyotes.

How do you become an oak or a bear? To walk fearless everywhere you choose to go?

Discipline.

You rise above the status quo. While others sit, you stand. While they sleep, you train. While they consume garbage, you feed your soul. While they stare idly into the blue light of their screens, you study the ancient ways and grow wiser. While they get fatter and slower in their modern comforts, you suffer joyously, and get harder, meaner and more resilient. When they frown and moan in hard times, you smile and laugh with joy in your heart because you know your purpose.

Fear is doubt. Fear is not being prepared. Fear is a weak, slow incapable body and undisciplined mind. Fear is ignorance and full of excuses. Fear is compromise.

Fear is human.

Escape.

The Wilderness calls to me. In the trees, below the canopy where the wild things dwell, where I can embrace the elements and forget that I am Human is where I am happiest. Where I can be myself, and rely on my own wits and brawn. Where I am no longer at the top of the food chain. That is true living; to be both predator and prey. Muscles matter. Common sense matters. Training matters. Your ability to thrive despite the glorious suffering matters. The wind, rain, heat, and the claws and teeth matter. Scar tissue, and calloused hands matter. Your feelings do not matter. Your politics do not matter. Your gender, and race do not matter. Your money does not matter. The Wilderness does not care about you. It is the last honest thing we have. I am also a modern human, and a realist. I have a job, and a car... bills, and responsibilities, but I also cannot ignore the pull of the wild that surrounds me. I am happiest when in it, whether in the middle of the trees, ocean, or the darkest brick laden bowels of the city. The wild is where the escape begins. **Wander. Stay busy. Let it all go. Focus on self-improvement. Be an asset to your society. Love children and animals. Be better.**

Made in the USA
Columbia, SC
13 December 2019